MW01064947

THE MAFIA JUST MOVED IN NEXT DOOR AND THEY'RE DROPPING BY FOR DINNER COOKBOOK

EASY ITALIAN RECIPES

MAFIA MAGICIAN.
THIS TRICK RARELY WORKS PROPERLY

LAGOON BOOKS

TYPICAL SCENE IN
'ITALIAN FAMILY CAFE'

PUBLISHED IN 2000 BY
LAGOON BOOKS
PO BOX 311, KT2 5QW, UK
PO BOX 990676, BOSTON, MA 02199, USA
WWW.LAGOONGAMES.COM

ISBN: 1902813154

FIRST PUBLISHED IN AUSTRALIA IN 1998 BY
PAN MACMILLAN AUSTRALIA PTY LIMITED

COPYRIGHT © 1998 BILLY BLUE MERCHANDISING PTY LTD

RECIPES BY HELEN TRACEY AND LINDA KAPLAN

ADDITIONAL WRITING BY ROSS RENWICK

SUPERVISING CHEFS MATT BLUNDELL AND GAVIN CUMMINS

OF KENTRA DOUBLE BAY AUSTRALIA

MANAGING DIRECTOR AARON KAPLAN   CREATIVE DIRECTOR ROSS RENWICK

PRINTED IN SINGAPORE

Italian man training Zabaglione.
Beware of more Zabaglione and
Gorgonzola jokes

LIARS

There are layers of liars.

But as far as I can tell there are two main types.

There are those people who lie to you for personal gain.

And there are those more charming liars who lie to amuse.

For example, if I told you that I had it on good authority that Bill Clinton has been dead for three years and the person you see is a robotic dummy supplied by the CIA so that the stockmarket won't fall, would you believe me?

And that Hillary, who was running the country in the background, has surrendered power to the behind-the-scenes triumvirate of Doris Day, Mike Tyson and Kevin Bacon.

And worse still for the American dream, the three of them are running America from three matching villas in Via Cavour in the east of Rome, and that there's a lot of heavy drinking and eating going on as Rome can be a lot of fun if you're drunk and running America at the same time.

As you can see from the structure of that last sentence, I've been drinking heavily too.

But back to business. Yesterday the three of them invited me to dinner and while Mike Tyson was making boxing commissions illegal and firing the joint chief of staff, I copied down the recipes.

Suspend your belief if you must, but the recipes are great.

POTATOES WITH BACON AND ROSEMARY

8 POTATOES

8 TABLESPOONS OLIVE OIL

4 RASHERS OF BACON, DICED

5 TABLESPOONS FRESH ROSEMARY

1 TABLESPOON LEMON JUICE

MIX INGREDIENTS IN A LARGE METAL BOWL.

TRANSFER TO A BAKING DISH.

COOK IN A PREHEATED MODERATE OVEN UNTIL THE POTATOES ARE COOKED THROUGH.

IRRELEVANT ILLUSTRATION

VALDA ZAIR

I am now living in Via Cavour across the road from the people who are running America.

The three people now running America after a complete stuff-up by the CIA are Doris Day, Mike Tyson and Kevin Bacon.

Kevin who would be king. Doris who likes Boris (Yeltsin) and Mike who rides a bike.

This is going nowhere, as you can guess, and it's a complete indictment of the system of paying a dollar a word. I mean the cat sat on the mat just earned me twenty-two dollars, and I'm not very good at counting earned me a few more still.

And if you're still reading this stuff, don't let on to the publisher, but I actually don't give a stuff because none us will ever see the publisher who probably lives on the south edge of Capri when it's warm and in the winter either screws Valda Zair or skis there.

Anyway, the next recipe is...

RISOTTO

RICE WITH PEAS
SERVES 6.

1kg/2lb FRESH PEAS
1 HANDFUL ITALIAN PARSLEY
3 TABLESPOONS OLIVE OIL
115g/4oz PANCETTA

180ml/$^3/_4$ CUP WHITE WINE
750ml/3 CUPS BEEF STOCK
400g/2 CUPS SHORT-GRAIN RICE
SALT AND PEPPER
4 TABLESPOONS UNSALTED BUTTER
FRESH GRATED PARMESAN

SHELL PEAS.

BOIL PODS IN 750ml/3 CUPS SALTED WATER
AND SIMMER FOR $1^1/_2$ HOURS.

HEAT OIL, ADD PANCETTA AND SAUTE 3 MINUTES.
ADD PARSLEY AND PEAS AND COOK OVER LOW HEAT
FOR 15 MINUTES. PEAS SHOULD BE FIRM BUT COOKED.

REMOVE AND LEAVE PEAS COVERED UNTIL NEEDED.

REMOVE PODS FROM WATER AND DISCARD.

POUR JUICES FROM COOKED PEAS INTO LARGE POT
AND BRING TO BOIL. ADD RICE AND SAUTE FOR 5
MINUTES. COMBINE PEA-POD WATER AND BEEF STOCK
AND HEAT. ADD GRADUALLY TO RICF, RETAINING
60ml/$^1/_4$ CUP, STIRRING GENTLY UNTIL MOST OF THE
LIQUID HAS BEEN ABSORBED.

ADD THE PEAS AND THE FINAL 60ml/$^1/_4$ CUP.
SEASON.
ADD BUTTER AND PARMESAN. SERVE IMMEDIATELY.

BEETHOVEN

I am sitting on Via Luigi gazing at the countryside outside Florence and idly tapping on the piano the 32 Beethoven sonatas - very difficult to play, especially on a verandah.

Why did Beethoven compose 32 sonatas? Has it anything to do with the fact that there are only 32 plots in literature?

How long is it since my waist measured 32 and will it ever again?

I can ask Beethoven in a few moments because he is coming to lunch. I hope that he doesn't play that game where he pretends to be deaf.

He has always wanted to meet Doris Day so I have invited her as well. Jimi Hendrix is coming and so is Nelson Mandela who comes to many of my lunches.

Beethoven, Doris Day, Jimi Hendrix and Nelson Mandela begs the question of what to serve.

A German, a white American woman, a black American man and a black South African.

Only a great Italian recipe could please them all. Here it is.

LAGUNA VENETA

BAKED FISH WITH HERBS
SERVES 4.

1 LARGE BABY SNAPPER
SALT AND CRACKED PEPPER
OLIVE OIL FOR BRUSHING

HANDFUL ITALIAN PARSLEY
¹/₂ BUNCH DILL
15 FRESH SAGE LEAVES
2 SPRIGS ROSEMARY
SMALL BUNCH OREGANO
10 LARGE BASIL LEAVES
125ml/¹/₂ CUP LEMON JUICE
125ml/¹/₂ CUP WHITE WINE

STUFFING:

1 LEMON, CUT IN QUARTERS
EXTRA BUNCH PARSLEY

WASH AND PAT FISH DRY.

STUFF WITH LEMON QUARTERS AND PARSLEY.

PLACE ON LARGE PIECE OF FOIL BRUSHED WITH OIL.

ROLL EDGES UP AND ADD LEMON JUICE, WINE, SALT, PEPPER AND HERBS.

WRAP FOIL COMPLETELY AROUND FISH AND PUT IN A BAKING DISH.

BAKE IN MODERATE OVEN FOR 20 MINUTES.

REMOVE AND STAND FOR 5 MINUTES BEFORE UNWRAPPING. SERVE IMMEDIATELY WITH BOILED POTATOES, GREEN SALAD AND CRUSTY BREAD.

GUARDS

I TOLD YOU ELSEWHERE THAT DORIS DAY, MIKE TYSON AND KEVIN BACON ARE ACTUALLY RUNNING AMERICA FROM THREE FETID ROMAN VILLAS AND THAT NO-ONE KNOWS THIS IS SO. EXCEPT ME, AND NOW YOU.

FOR SOME THIS MAY BE ENCOURAGING NEWS UNTIL YOU START RUMINATING ON MIKE TYSON BEING IN CHARGE OF THE ARMED FORCES OF THE UNITED STATES OF AMERICA.

IN QUEST OF BETTER AND BETTER RECIPES, I BEGAN TALKING TO THE THREE SECURITY PEOPLE WHO ARE IN CHARGE OF THE VILLAS OF THE PEOPLE RUNNING AMERICA.

THEY USUALLY SIT IN THE SUN PLAYING DICE AT A SMALL TABLE ON THE STREET.

FROM A SECURITY POINT OF VIEW THEIR INDOLENCE IS PERFECT AS WATCHFUL THIEVES ARE UNLIKELY TO BELIEVE THAT ANYTHING THIS LOT ARE GUARDING COULD BE OF VALUE.

JUT, ONE OF THE GUARDS WHO SAT IN THE SUN AND CONTINUALLY COMPLAINS ABOUT HIS LOSING FOOTBALL TEAM, COOKED THE MEAL OF THE CENTURY ON THE DAY THAT MIKE TYSON APPOINTED DON KING TO THE SUPREME COURT AND KEVIN BACON PASSED LEGISLATION THAT GAVE FILMMAKERS HUGE TAX DEDUCTIONS IF HE WAS THE LEAD ACTOR. JUT, AMIDST THIS LUNACY, COOKED THE MEAL OF THE CENTURY. I SHARE IT WITH YOU HERE.

ROAST CHICKEN WITH LEMON AND GARLIC

2 CHICKENS

6 LEMONS, HALVED

2 CLOVES GARLIC, FINELY CHOPPED
1 HANDFUL PARSLEY, CHOPPED
SALT AND CRACKED PEPPER
$\frac{1}{2}$ TEASPOON PAPRIKA
24 CLOVES GARLIC, UNPEELED

WASH THE CHICKENS AND RUB WITH SALT.

CUT IN HALF THROUGH BREASTBONE IN ORDER TO LIE CHICKEN OUT FLAT (ONLY CUT THROUGH THE ONE SIDE).

PLACE CHICKENS IN LARGE BOWL AND SQUEEZE WITH THE JUICE FROM LEMON HALVES.

ADD LEMONS TO THE BOWL.

ADD OTHER INGREDIENTS (EXCEPT UNPEELED GARLIC CLOVES) AND MIX THROUGH GENTLY.

MARINATE FOR 2 HOURS OR MORE, TURNING OCCASIONALLY.

PREHEAT OVEN TO HIGH. PLACE CHICKENS IN A LARGE BAKING DISH, SIDE BY SIDE, AND POUR OVER MARINADE.

LIE LEMON HALVES UPSIDE DOWN ON CHICKENS, AND PLACE GARLIC CLOVES AROUND EDGES. COOK FOR 45 MINUTES.

TEST BY STICKING A SKEWER INTO THE THIGH – IF THE FLUID IS CLEAR, THE CHICKEN IS COOKED.

SERVE WITH LEMON HALVES ON TOP AND 4 CLOVES OF ROASTED GARLIC EACH.

TO EAT ROASTED GARLIC, PEEL OFF OUTER LAYER AND RETRIEVE PASTE.

PLUM TOMATO SALAD
PLUM TOMATOES (2 PER PERSON)
OLIVE OIL
ITALIAN BREAD
PROVOLONE CHEESE

WASH, DRY AND CUT THE TOMATOES IN HALF, DRIZZLE WITH OLIVE OIL.

PUT IN SLOW OVEN ON BAKING TRAY FOR 3 HOURS.

PUT IN BOWL, ADD MORE OLIVE OIL.

SERVE WITH CRUSTY ITALIAN BREAD, PROVOLONE CHEESE.

KEEPS WELL IN FRIDGE COVERED WITH CLING WRAP UP TO 1 WEEK.

GOOD AL FRESCO LUNCH. SERVE WITH BOTTLE OF CHILLED FRASCATI.

VARIATIONS: CHOP IN 1 CLOVE GARLIC, ADD SALT AND PEPPER.

ADD CHOPPED BASIL.

USE A POTATO PEELER TO SLICE ZUCCHINI, FRY WITH OLIVE OIL AND GARLIC, SERVE WITH TOMATOES, BREAD AND CHEESE.

CAPSICUM SALAD AND CAPERS

4 CAPSICUMS – A COMBINATION OF GREEN, RED AND YELLOW
1 ONION, SLICED
1 CLOVE GARLIC, FINELY CHOPPED
6 LARGE BASIL LEAVES, SHREDDED
2 TABLESPOONS CAPERS
1 CAN ITALIAN TOMATOES
1 TABLESPOON TOMATO PASTE
60ml/$^1/_4$ CUP OLIVE OIL
SALT AND PEPPER

PREHEAT OVEN TO MEDIUM.

PUT CAPSICUMS ON OVEN SHELF AND CHAR SLIGHTLY ON ALL SIDES.

REMOVE TO PLASTIC BAG AND LET STAND FOR 30 MINUTES.

FRY GARLIC FOR 3 MINUTES IN OLIVE OIL.

ADD ONION, COOK UNTIL OPAQUE.

ADD TOMATOES AND SIMMER FOR 5 MINUTES.

ADD TOMATO PASTE. ALLOW TO SIMMER UNTIL SLIGHTLY THICK IN TEXTURE.

ADD SALT AND PEPPER.

PEEL CAPSICUMS AND CUT INTO FINE STRIPS. PLACE ON A LARGE SERVING PLATE.

ADD BASIL TO TOMATO SAUCE AND POUR OVER CAPSICUMS.

SPRINKLE CAPERS ON TOP. SERVE WITH CRUSTY BREAD.

BAKED EGGPLANT

2 LARGE ROUND EGGPLANTS/AUBERGINES
3 CLOVES GARLIC, DICED
4 TABLESPOONS OLIVE OIL
SALT AND PEPPER
SPRIGS OF ITALIAN PARSLEY

CUT THE EGGPLANTS INTO ROUNDS,
ABOUT 2cm THICK.

SALT LIBERALLY.

ALLOW TO STAND $1/2$ HOUR.

PREHEAT OVEN TO 190°C/375°F/GAS MARK 5.

OIL BAKING DISH.

RINSE OFF EGGPLANT AND PAT DRY.

PLACE SIDE BY SIDE IN DISH AND SPRINKLE A FEW
PIECES OF GARLIC ON EACH EGGPLANT.

POUR REST OF OIL OVER EGGPLANT AND BAKE
FOR 25 MINUTES.

PUT ON SERVING PLATTER, SPRINKLE WITH PARSLEY,
ADD SALT AND PEPPER.

SERVE WITH BREAD AND/OR CHEESE.

CAN BE ADDED TO ANTIPASTO OR SERVED
WITH A MAIN DISH.

CANNELLINI BEANS WITH ROSEMARY

400g/2 CUPS DRIED CANNELLINI BEANS
85g/3oz PANCETTA
4 TABLESPOONS OLIVE OIL
3 CLOVES GARLIC, FINELY CHOPPED
3 TABLESPOONS FRESH ROSEMARY
SALT AND PEPPER

SOAK BEANS OVERNIGHT.

DRAIN AND RINSE THE NEXT DAY.

PUT IN CASSEROLE DISH WITH OTHER INGREDIENTS.

COVER WITH WATER; BEANS MUST BE WELL COVERED,
WITH WATER COMING ABOUT $2^1/_2$ cm OVER BEANS.

PLACE IN A PREHEATED MODERATE OVEN.

BAKE $1^1/_2$ HOURS, STIRRING A FEW TIMES.

ADD SALT AND PEPPER.

REMOVE AND LET STAND FOR 15 MINUTES BEFORE
SERVING.

EYE PATCH WORN BY KEVIN BACON WHILE
PRACTISING SINGING 'THREE COINS IN THE
FOUNTAIN' IN FRONT OF THE MIRROR

GLAZED ONIONS

500g/1lb PICKLING ONIONS
3 TABLESPOONS OLIVE OIL
3 TABLESPOONS TARRAGON VINEGAR
2 TABLESPOONS SUGAR
2 BAY LEAVES
SPRIG OF OREGANO

BOIL UNPEELED ONIONS FOR 5 MINUTES.

REMOVE FROM WATER AND CAREFULLY PEEL.

PLACE OIL, VINEGAR, SUGAR AND HERBS
IN SAUCEPAN.

ADD ONIONS. COVER AND SIMMER 15 MINUTES
OR UNTIL TENDER AND CARAMELLY. SEASON.

FAMOUS ITALIAN RESTAURANT ALSO
KNOWN FOR ITS GLAZED ONIONS

MARINATED MUSHROOMS

500g/1lb BUTTON MUSHROOMS, THINLY SLICED

125ml/$^1/_2$ CUP EXTRA VIRGIN OLIVE OIL

DASH OF WHITE WINE VINEGAR

2 TABLESPOONS LEMON JUICE

CHOPPED PARSLEY

1 GARLIC CLOVE, FINELY CHOPPED

SALT AND PEPPER

WASH AND DRY MUSHROOMS WELL.

COMBINE DRESSING INGREDIENTS, MIXING WELL (WITH A FORK OR WHISK), POUR OVER MUSHROOMS AND STIR THROUGH.

COVER AND LEAVE TO MARINATE OVERNIGHT.

TYPICAL ITALIAN PIZZA SHOP

SOUPS

MINESTRONE

USE A COMBINATION OF DICED VEGETABLES INCLUDING:

1 ONION, 1 CARROT, 3 ZUCCHINI, 400g/ 2 CUPS OF HARICOT BEANS, 2 CELERY STALKS, SAVOY CABBAGE, SHREDDED, 4 LARGE RIPE TOMATOES, 1 FENNEL BULB, BROCCOLI, CAULIFLOWER

125ml/$^1/_2$ CUP OIL

2 TABLESPOONS BUTTER

3 BEEF STOCK CUBES

1 TABLESPOON OLIVE OIL

1 CLOVE GARLIC, DICED

SALT AND PEPPER

2 400g/14oz CANS TOMATOES

FRESH PARMESAN CHEESE

COMBINE OIL AND BUTTER.

FRY THE VEGETABLES, STARTING WITH THE ONION, AND GRADUALLY ADDING THE OTHERS.

ADD 1 LITRE/ $1^3/_4$ PINTS WATER AND STOCK CUBES.

BOIL, THEN SIMMER FOR 2 HOURS. IN A FRYPAN, HEAT A LITTLE OLIVE OIL AND FRY DICED GARLIC CLOVE FOR 30 SECONDS.

ADD A GENEROUS AMOUNT OF SALT AND PEPPER AND THE CANS OF TOMATOES. SIMMER FOR 20 MINUTES.

ADD TO SOUP AND CONTINUE COOKING UNTIL SOUP IS DESIRED THICKNESS.

SERVE WITH CRUSTY BREAD AND GRATED FRESH PARMESAN CHEESE.

LENTIL SOUP

1 ONION

2 STICKS CELERY

2 CARROTS

1 FENNEL BULB

500g/1lb SPINACH, SHREDDED

15g/$^1/_2$oz BUTTER

1 TABLESPOON OIL

250g/9oz BACON OR HAM BONES

250g/9oz LENTILS

1 400g/14oz CAN TOMATOES

1 LITRE/4 CUPS WATER

2 BEEF STOCK CUBES

PEPPER

2 TABLESPOONS CHOPPED PARSLEY

6 MARJORAM LEAVES, CHOPPED

FINELY DICE VEGETABLES AND FRY IN MIXTURE OF OIL AND BUTTER. ADD BACON OR HAM BONES, LENTILS, CANNED TOMATOES, MARJORAM LEAVES, WATER AND STOCK CUBES. COVER, BRING TO THE BOIL.

REDUCE HEAT AND SIMMER $1^1/_2$ HOURS OR UNTIL LENTILS ARE TENDER. REMOVE BONES, SPRINKLE WITH PARSLEY AND PEPPER AND SERVE WITH CRUSTY BREAD.

FISH SOUP

**2kg/4lb ASSORTED FISH
(MULLET, ROCK COD, WHITING)**

**FISH BONES FROM WHITE FISH
(E.G. SNAPPER)**

1/2 LEMON

**3 LARGE RIPE TOMATOES, PEELED
AND CHOPPED**

SALT AND PEPPER

125ml/1/2 CUP OLIVE OIL

2 CLOVES GARLIC, FINELY CHOPPED

1 MEDIUM ONION, FINELY CHOPPED

6 SPRIGS PARSLEY, FINELY CHOPPED

**6 SLICES BREAD, FRIED IN
GARLIC-FLAVOURED OIL**

GRATED FRESH PARMESAN OR PECORINO

ASK THE FISHMONGER TO REMOVE FILLETS AND RETAIN BONES FOR STOCK. (MY FISHMONGER WOULD TELL ME TO GET STUFFED.)

PLACE BONES AND HEADS IN A LARGE POT.

ADD LEMON AND TOMATOES AND COVER WITH 2 LITRES/3 1/2 PINTS OF WATER.

BRING TO THE BOIL, TURN DOWN TO SIMMER AND COOK OVER A MODERATE HEAT FOR 30 MINUTES, SKIMMING UNTIL CLEAR.

STRAIN AND RETAIN THE STOCK.

IN ANOTHER POT, SAUTE GARLIC, ONION AND PARSLEY IN OIL UNTIL ONION IS GOLDEN.

ADD THE FISH FILLETS.

WHEN COOKED (WHEN FISH TURNS FROM OPAQUE TO WHITE), ADD THE STOCK AND SALT AND PEPPER.

BRING TO THE BOIL.

PLACE ONE PIECE OF FRIED BREAD IN EACH SOUP BOWL, SPRINKLE WITH CHEESE AND LADLE SOUP OVER THE TOP. SERVE IMMEDIATELY.

SPECIAL MAP TO FIND POLITE FISHMONGER

STRACCIATELLA

2 CHICKEN LEGS AND THIGHS

2 STICKS CELERY

2 CARROTS

1 ONION

1 TEASPOON BLACK PEPPERCORNS

$1/2$ BUNCH ITALIAN PARSLEY

1 CLOVE GARLIC

SALT AND PEPPER

$1^1/2$ LITRES/$2^1/2$ PINTS WATER

3 EGGS

3 TABLESPOONS FINE BREADCRUMBS

PARMESAN OR PECORINO CHEESE, FRESHLY GRATED

COMBINE FIRST 8 INGREDIENTS, ROUGHLY CHOPPED, IN A SAUCEPAN. ADD WATER.

BOIL, THEN REDUCE HEAT AND SIMMER 50 MINUTES. STRAIN, RESERVING STOCK.

BEAT EGGS, PARSLEY, BREADCRUMBS AND CHEESE TOGETHER.

BRING STOCK TO BOIL.

ADD A LITTLE BOILING STOCK TO THE EGG MIX, BEATING WELL. THEN ADD GRADUALLY TO THE STOCK, BEATING VIGOROUSLY. SERVE IMMEDIATELY.

SPRING VEGETABLES

2 BUNCHES ASPARAGUS

200g/7oz GREEN BEANS

1 PACKET SNOW PEAS

1 WHITE ONION, SLICED

1 CARROT, CUT IN JULIENNE STRIPS

1 ZUCCHINI, CUT IN JULIENNE STRIPS

**200g/7oz BUTTON MUSHROOMS,
FINELY SLICED**

4 PLUM TOMATOES

OLIVE OIL

1 CLOVE GARLIC, CHOPPED

SALT AND CRACKED PEPPER

1 HANDFUL ITALIAN PARSLEY

SPRIGS OF FRESH BASIL

HEAT OIL, ADD GARLIC AND COOK 2 MINUTES.

ADD ONION, CARROT, ZUCCHINI, MUSHROOMS
AND COOK 5 MINUTES.

ADD ASPARAGUS, BEANS AND SNOW PEAS TO
BOILING WATER FOR 30 SECONDS. REFRESH.

ADD TO FRYPAN WITH TOMATOES, SALT AND PEPPER.
COOK 10-15 MINUTES.

ADD PARSLEY AND BASIL.

MUSSELS AND TOMATOES

1kg/2lb LOCAL (BLACK) MUSSELS
1 ONION, SLICED
3 CLOVES GARLIC, FINELY CHOPPED
3 TABLESPOONS OLIVE OIL
1/2 BUNCH ITALIAN PARSLEY, CHOPPED
1 CAN ITALIAN TOMATOES
SALT AND PEPPER
125ml/1/2 CUP WHITE WINE

GENTLY FRY ONION IN OLIVE OIL UNTIL TRANSLUCENT.

ADD GARLIC, TOMATOES, SALT AND PEPPER AND
WHITE WINE.

COOK 5 MINUTES, ADD SCRUBBED
AND DEBEARDED MUSSELS AND PARSLEY.

COOK UNTIL MUSSELS OPEN.

SERVE WITH CRUSTY BREAD AND A GREEN SALAD.

THIRTY SMALL TOMATOES

PASTA SAUCES

SICILIAN

1 BROWN ONION, FINELY CHOPPED
1 SMALL EGGPLANT, CUT INTO CUBES
1 GREEN CAPSICUM
1kg/2lb LOCAL (BLACK) MUSSELS
3 CLOVES GARLIC, FINELY CHOPPED
3 TABLESPOONS OLIVE OIL
$1/2$ BUNCH ITALIAN PARSLEY, CHOPPED
1 CAN ITALIAN TOMATOES
SALT AND PEPPER
125ml/$1/2$ CUP WHITE WINE

GENTLY FRY ONION IN OLIVE OIL UNTIL TRANSLUCENT.

ADD GARLIC, EGGPLANT, CAPSICUM, TOMATOES, SALT AND PEPPER AND WHITE WINE.

COOK 5 MINUTES, ADD SCRUBBED AND DEBEARDED MUSSELS AND PARSLEY. COOK UNTIL MUSSELS OPEN.

SERVE WITH CRUSTY BREAD AND GREEN SALAD.

GORGONZOLA

125g/5oz GORGONZOLA, CHOPPED
125ml/¹⁄₂ CUP MILK
1 TABLESPOON BUTTER
SALT AND PEPPER
2 TABLESPOONS CREAM

COMBINE GORGONZOLA, MILK, BUTTER AND
SALT AND PEPPER IN LARGE FRYPAN.

PLACE ON GENTLE HEAT.

COOK, STIRRING UNTIL SMOOTH AND CREAMY.

ADD CREAM AND STIR UNTIL SAUCE THICKENS.

STIR THROUGH PASTA.

DO NOT USE LAWN MOWER TO MIX GORGONZOLA.
GORGONZOLA IS NOT RELATED TO EMIL ZOLA

SMOKED SALMON

SMOKED SALMON
1 TABLESPOON FRESH DILL, CHOPPED
2 TABLESPOONS PARSLEY,
CHOPPED PEPPER

BOIL PASTA, DRAIN, AND STIR BUTTER THROUGH IT.

ADD THIN STRIPS OF SMOKED SALMON, FRESH DILL
AND FRESH PARSLEY.

TOSS, ADD A GOOD QUANTITY OF PEPPER AND SERVE
STRAIGHTAWAY WITH CRISP GREEN SALAD.

Salmon smoking

OIL, GARLIC, CHILLI AND BASIL

4 TABLESPOONS EXTRA VIRGIN OLIVE OIL

2 CLOVES GARLIC, FINELY CHOPPED

5 TABLESPOONS BASIL

1 SMALL CHILLI, FINELY CHOPPED

HEAT OIL AND FRY GARLIC AND CHILLI TO WARM.

ADD BASIL AND STIR THROUGH THOROUGHLY.
STIR SAUCE THROUGH PASTA.

UNDERPANTS CAPTIONS
HAVE BEEN FORBIDDEN BY THE PUBLISHER

PESTO

THIS ONE'S REALLY EASY, AS YOU CAN TAKE A REAL
SHORT CUT AND BUY A JAR OF PESTO TO STIR
THROUGH THE PASTA – IT TASTES ALMOST AS GOOD
AS HOMEMADE. IF YOU WANT TO MAKE YOUR OWN,
HOWEVER, YOU NEED:

4 BUNCHES FRESH BASIL

2 TABLESPOONS PINE NUTS

2 CLOVES GARLIC

SALT AND CRACKED PEPPER

250ml/1 CUP OLIVE OIL

3 TABLESPOONS GRATED PARMESAN

3 TABLESPOONS PECORINO

TOAST PINE NUTS IN PAN UNTIL GOLDEN BROWN.

BLEND BASIL, PINE NUTS, GARLIC, SALT AND PEPPER
UNTIL SMOOTH.

ADD OIL IN THIN STREAM, SLOWLY, UNTIL WELL MIXED.

PLACE IN BOWL AND STIR PARMESAN AND
PECORINO THROUGH.

MARINARA

4 TABLESPOONS EXTRA VIRGIN OLIVE OIL
8 CLOVES GARLIC, PEELED
$1/_4$ TEASPOON CHILLI FLAKES
SALT
1 CAN PEELED PLUM TOMATOES
250ml/1 CUP DRY WHITE WINE
10 CONTINENTAL PARSLEY SPRIGS
GROUND BLACK PEPPER TO TASTE
500g/1lb CLAMS
500g/1lb FRESH MUSSELS
500g/1lb FRESH PRAWNS

HEAT OIL, GARLIC, CHILLI FLAKES AND A PINCH OF SALT.

STIR UNTIL GARLIC IS GOLDEN.

ADD PUREED TOMATOES.

STIR AND SIMMER UNTIL SAUCE THICKENS AND GARLIC IS TENDER.

SCRUB THE MUSSELS AND RINSE UNDER WATER.

DISCARD ANY OPENED MUSSELS.

IN A LARGE PAN, PLACE THE MUSSELS, PARSLEY AND HALF THE WINE.

COOK COVERED UNTIL MUSSELS OPEN.

DO NOT OVERCOOK; DISCARD ANY
UNOPENED MUSSELS.

STRAIN WINE INTO TOMATO SAUCE AND
REMOVE MUSSELS TO SERVING BOWL.

KEEP WARM.

REPEAT MUSSEL PROCESS WITH CLAMS.

TASTE SAUCE AND CORRECT THE SEASONING.

REDUCE SAUCE FURTHER IF IT IS TOO THIN.

SAUTE PRAWNS IN 1 TABLESPOON OF OIL
UNTIL COOKED.

ADD ALL SEAFOOD TO TOMATO SAUCE AND STIR.

SERVE WITH YOUR FAVOURITE PASTA.

A LICENCE IS REQUIRED TO MAKE MARINARA.
SEND ME $50 IN UNMARKED BILLS
AND I'LL SEND YOU ONE

RICE CROQUETTES WITH CHEESE FILLING

300g/1 1/2 CUPS RISOTTO RICE
50g/1/2 CUP GRATED PARMESAN
2 EGGS
140g/1 CUP FINE DRY BREADCRUMBS
OIL FOR DEEP FRYING

COOK RICE AS FOR THE RISOTTO RECIPE ON PAGE 8 UNTIL TENDER AND DRY. ADD THE GRATED PARMESAN CHEESE AND 1 EGG.

FILLING:
50g/1/2 CUP CUBED MOZZARELLA CHEESE

TAKE SMALL PORTIONS OF THE RICE AND FORM BALL SHAPES. MAKE A HOLE IN THE CENTRE OF EACH BALL USING YOUR THUMB. PLACE 1 CUBE OF DICED MOZZARELLA INTO EACH HOLE. SMOOTH OVER THE OPENING TO ENCLOSE THE CHEESE. DIP THE BALLS INTO 1 BEATEN EGG AND ROLL IN BREADCRUMBS. USE MORE EGGS AND BREADCRUMBS IF NECESSARY. DEEP-FRY IN HOT OIL UNTIL GOLDEN ALL OVER.

SERVE WITH GREEN SALAD. CAN BE SERVED AS AN ENTREE OR MAIN COURSE.

THE SALAD TO SERVE WITH
ANYTHING AND EVERYTHING

CHOOSE YOUR FAVOURITE SALAD LEAVES
– ROCKET, MESCLUN, ICEBERG

DRESS WITH OLIVE OIL AND YOUR CHOICE
OF VINEGAR (AT A RATIO OF 3:1). IF USING
BALSAMIC VINEGAR, THE RATIO IS 5:1.

ADD A SQUEEZE OF LEMON IF DESIRED,
AND SALT AND PEPPER.

SHAKE WELL. POUR OVER LETTUCE.

ACTUAL PHOTOGRAPH OF THE AUTHOR
(IRRELEVANT)

TROUT WITH ENGLISH SPINACH AND LOCAL MUSSELS

1 RAINBOW TROUT PER PERSON

1/2 kg/1 lb LOCAL (BLACK) MUSSELS

1 BUNCH ENGLISH SPINACH

JUICE 2 LEMONS

COARSE SALT

2 GLASSES WHITE WINE

DEBEARD MUSSELS AND REMOVE FROM SHELLS.

DEBONE TROUT.

RUB INSIDE WITH SALT AND STUFF WITH 4-5 MUSSELS AND 6 SPINACH LEAVES.

ADD A LITTLE LEMON JUICE.

LIE TROUT SIDE BY SIDE IN BAKING DISH.

POUR OVER WINE.

BAKE IN MODERATE OVEN FOR 20 MINUTES, OR UNTIL COOKED THROUGH.

SERVE WITH SNOW PEAS AND WILD RICE.

MEAT

CARPACCIO

400g/14oz BEEF STRIPLOIN, TRIMMED
JUICE 3 LEMONS
1 CLOVE GARLIC, FINELY CHOPPED
125ml/$\frac{1}{2}$ CUP OLIVE OIL
SALT AND CRACKED BLACK PEPPER
SPRIGS ITALIAN PARSLEY
SHAVED PARMESAN

PLACE BEEF IN FREEZER FOR HALF AN HOUR TO FIRM, CUT INTO THIN SLICES WITH SHARP KNIFE.

MIX LEMON JUICE, GARLIC, OIL, SALT AND PEPPER.

SPREAD BEEF SLICES ON SERVING PLATE, POUR DRESSING OVER THE TOP.

ADD PARSLEY SPRIGS AND SHAVED PARMESAN.

AUTHOR AS SEEN BY HIMSELF
(IRRELEVANT)

VEAL WITH LEMON

12 SMALL VEAL SCALOPPINE
FLOUR FOR DUSTING
200g/7oz SLICED MUSHROOMS
6 TABLESPOONS BUTTER
SALT AND PEPPER
PARSLEY, FINELY CHOPPED
JUICE 1 LEMON
125ml/1/2 CUP HOT CHICKEN STOCK

BEAT SCALOPPINE UNTIL THIN.

SPRINKLE WITH FLOUR.

HEAT 3 TABLESPOONS OF BUTTER, ADD VEAL.

FRY QUICKLY UNTIL LIGHTLY BROWNED.

SEASON LIGHTLY.

REMOVE FROM HEAT, ADD MUSHROOMS AND A FURTHER 2 TABLESPOONS BUTTER AND SAUTE BRIEFLY.

SEASON.

ADD PARSLEY, LEMON JUICE AND THE REMAINING BUTTER AND STOCK. STIR.

WHEN HOT, POUR OVER VEAL.

SERVE WITH BOILED POTATOES GARNISHED WITH CHOPPED PARSLEY.

SALTIMBOCCA

VEAL SCALOPPINE WITH PANCETTA
AND SAGE.

**8 MEDIUM VEAL SCALOPPINE
(2 PER PERSON)**

8 SLICES OF PANCETTA OR PROSCIUTTO

8 FRESH SAGE LEAVES

50g/2oz BUTTER

SALT AND PEPPER

125ml/$\frac{1}{2}$ CUP DRY WHITE WINE

PLACE CLING WRAP UNDER AND OVER
THE SLICES OF VEAL.

BEAT THE MEAT WITH A MALLET UNTIL THIN.

PLACE PANCETTA OR PROSCIUTTO AND A
SAGE LEAF ON TOP.

SECURE WITH A TOOTHPICK.

MELT BUTTER IN A LARGE PAN AND ADD VEAL.

BROWN ON BOTH SIDES.

SEASON LIGHTLY WITH SALT AND PEPPER.

MOISTEN WITH WINE.

TOTAL COOKING TIME SHOULD BE LESS THAN
5 MINUTES.

REMOVE TO SERVING DISH AND POUR SAUCE
OVER THE TOP.

CHICKEN WITH TOMATOES AND MUSHROOMS

4 180g/6oz CHICKEN BREAST FILLETS
100g/4oz SLICED BUTTON MUSHROOMS
60ml/¼ CUP OLIVE OIL
1 CLOVE GARLIC, CRUSHED
4 SLICES OF PANCETTA
1 MEDIUM ONION, FINELY CHOPPED
125ml/½ CUP DRY WHITE WINE
SALT AND PEPPER
1 400g/14oz CAN TOMATOES
2 SPRIGS OF PARSLEY

HEAT OIL.

GENTLY BROWN THE CHICKEN WITH THE GARLIC, PANCETTA AND ONION.

WHEN THE GARLIC BEGINS TO BROWN, DISCARD IT AND ADD WHITE WINE.

SEASON WITH SALT AND PEPPER.

ADD MUSHROOMS, TOMATOES AND PARSLEY.

COOK UNTIL TENDER.

THE SAUCE SHOULD BE REASONABLY THICK.

THIN WITH CHICKEN STOCK OR WATER IF NECESSARY

GRILLED SPATCHCOCK

1 SPATCHCOCK PER PERSON

MARINATE IN:

JUICE 1 LEMON
60ml/$\frac{1}{4}$ CUP OLIVE OIL
6 SPRIGS FRESH OREGANO
SALT AND PEPPER
3 CLOVES GARLIC, CRUSHED

MARINATE SPATCHCOCK FOR 1 HOUR OR MORE.

HEAT GRILLER ON HIGH. GRILL, SKIN-SIDE TO THE HEAT.

TURN AFTER 8 MINUTES, BASTING WITH THE
REMAINING MARINADE.

GRILL FOR A FURTHER 5 MINUTES.

TEST WITH A SKEWER IN THIGH MEAT; WHEN
COOKED THE FLUID WILL RUN CLEAR.

SERVE WITH ROCKET SALAD DRESSED WITH OLIVE OIL
AND BALSAMIC VINEGAR (AT A RATIO OF 5:1, SHAKEN
EXTREMELY WELL).

SEAFOOD

BABY OCTOPUS SALAD

1 1/2kg/3lb BABY OCTOPUS

WHEN BUYING YOUR OCTOPUS, ASK YOUR
FISHMONGER FOR THE FRESHEST AVAILABLE. THEY
MUST BE SHINY AND SMELL OF THE SEA (AVOID ACRID-
SMELLING OCTOPUS).
IN ADDITION ASK FOR TENDERISED OCTOPUS. TO
CLEAN, TURN HEAD OF THE OCTOPUS INSIDE OUT
AND EMPTY. TAKE CARE TO AVOID RUPTURING THE INK-
SAC. REMOVE AND DISCARD THE EYE AND BEAK AT
THE BOTTOM OF THE HEAD. RETAIN AND USE THE
TENTACLES. RINSE.

PLACE THE OCTOPUS IN A LARGE POT AND
COVER WITH WATER.

LIGHTLY SALT.

BRING TO THE BOIL SLOWLY.

SIMMER FOR 1 HOUR, CHECKING FOR TENDERNESS.
NOTE THAT LARGER OCTOPUS TAKE LONGER TO
COOK; SMALLER TAKE LESS TIME.

REMOVE FROM THE WATER.

POUR THE DRESSING OVER THE OCTOPUS WHILE STILL
HOT AND SERVE WARM OR COLD.

SERVE WITH A SIDE SALAD AND CRUSTY BREAD AS AN
ENTREE OR MAIN COURSE.

DRESSING:

8 TABLESPOONS OLIVE OIL

3 TABLESPOONS LEMON JUICE

1 CLOVE GARLIC, FINELY CHOPPED

4 SPRIGS PARSLEY, FINELY CHOPPED

SALT AND PEPPER

AUTHOR AS SEEN BY HIS WIVES
(IRRELEVANT)

VEGETABLES TO SERVE WITH MEAT AND FISH DISHES

GREEN BEANS WITH CRACKED PEPPER AND PARMESAN

½kg/1lb GREEN BEANS
BUTTER
CRACKED PEPPER
GRATED PARMESAN

TOP AND TAIL BEANS. BLANCH FOR 20 SECONDS IN BOILING WATER AND REFRESH IN COLD WATER.

MELT THE BUTTER.

ADD THE BEANS TO THE HEAT AND TOSS FOR 20 SECONDS.

ADD PEPPER, SALT AND PARMESAN.

REMOVE FROM PAN AND PLACE ON A WARMED SERVING DISH.

POTATOES WITH PARMESAN

8 PONTIAC POTATOES
CHICKEN STOCK
FRESHLY GRATED PARMESAN CHEESE
SALT AND CRACKED PEPPER
CHOPPED PARSLEY

PREHEAT OVEN TO 150°C/300°F/GAS MARK 2.
PEEL AND SLICE THE POTATOES.

LIE POTATOES IN A BAKING DISH, SIDE BY SIDE,
COVERING THE BOTTOM OF THE DISH.

BOIL CHICKEN STOCK (ENOUGH TO
COVER POTATOES).

POUR ON TOP OF THE POTATOES.

COVER WITH PARMESAN, SALT AND PEPPER.

PUT IN THE OVEN AND BAKE UNTIL COOKED,
TURN THE OVEN TO HIGH AND BROWN.

GARNISH WITH CHOPPED PARSLEY.

Meeting chaired by Boris Yeltsin
that decided you would not have
heard of Pontiac potatoes unless you
were Californian

DESSERTS
STUFFED PEACHES

6 LARGE PEACHES, RIPE BUT FIRM
180ml/$^3/_4$ CUP WHITE WINE
1 NIP COGNAC

STUFFING:
100g/$^1/_2$ CUP DARK COOKING CHOCOLATE
4 DESSERTSPOONS BUTTER
1 NIP GRAND MARNIER
2 EGG YOLKS
$^1/_4$ TEASPOON VANILLA ESSENCE
1 DESSERTSPOON ICING SUGAR
180ml/$^3/_4$ CUP DOUBLE CREAM
1 TABLESPOON WHITE SUGAR
6 LARGE MERINGUES

WASH THE PEACHES AND PLACE IN A BOWL WITH THE WHITE WINE AND COGNAC.

ADD WATER UNTIL PEACHES ARE COMPLETELY COVERED.

LET STAND FOR 1 HOUR.

BREAK THE CHOCOLATE INTO PIECES AND PLACE IN A METAL BOWL.

BRING A POT OF WATER TO THE BOIL AND REDUCE HEAT TO A SIMMER. STAND THE BOWL WITH

CHOCOLATE OVER THE POT UNTIL THE CHOCOLATE HAS MELTED. ADD THE BUTTER AND STIR UNTIL WELL BLENDED.

REMOVE FROM THE HEAT.

CONTINUE STIRRING FOR A COUPLE OF MINUTES.

ADD THE EGG YOLKS, STIRRING (ALWAYS IN THE SAME DIRECTION) WITH A WOODEN SPOON UNTIL THE CHOCOLATE IS CREAMY AND ALMOST FLUFFY.

ADD THE GRAND MARNIER AND VANILLA ESSENCE AND STIR THROUGH.

WHIP THE CREAM WITH THE TWO LOTS OF SUGAR UNTIL WELL MIXED.

FOLD INTO THE CHOCOLATE MIXTURE.

REMOVE THE PEACHES FROM THE MARINADE AND CUT THE TOP $1^1/_2$ cm OFF.

CHECK THE PEACHES STAND LEVEL – IF THEY DON'T, REMOVE A SMALL PORTION FROM THE BOTTOM. CAREFULLY REMOVE THE PIP WITHOUT CUTTING INTO THE SIDES OR BOTTOM OF THE PEACH.

SPOON THE STUFFING INTO THE PIP CAVITY OF EACH PEACH, ALLOWING A SMALL AMOUNT OF THE MIXTURE TO SHOW ABOVE THE TOP OF THE PEACH.

SIT A MERINGUE ON TOP OF EACH PEACH AND PLACE ON A SERVING DISH.

IF NOT SERVING IMMEDIATELY, REFRIGERATE UNTIL NEEDED.

STUFFING CAN BE MADE THE DAY BEFORE USING AND PEACHES CAN BE STUFFED 2-3 HOURS BEFORE SERVING.

FIGS WITH RUM AND MASCARPONE

FOR THE FIGS:
500g/1lb FIGS (SLIGHTLY UNDERRIPE)
125g/4oz CASTOR SUGAR
60ml/$\frac{1}{4}$ CUP WATER
4 TABLESPOONS RUM

FOR THE MASCARPONE:
500g/1lb MASCARPONE
100g/4oz CASTOR SUGAR
4 EGG YOLKS
125ml/$\frac{1}{2}$ CUP RUM

RINSE FIGS AND DRAIN IN A COLANDER.

IN A POT, DISSOLVE SUGAR IN THE WATER.

ADD THE FIGS AND SIMMER WITH A LID ON
FOR 45 MINUTES OR UNTIL TENDER.

ADD RUM.

CAREFULLY REMOVE TO A BOWL AND ALLOW TO
COOL IN THE SYRUP.

MIX THE MASCARPONE AND CASTOR SUGAR AND
ADD THE YOLKS ONE AT A TIME.

CONTINUE BEATING WHILE ADDING THE RUM.

CHILL.

SERVE IN A BOWL WITH THE FIGS AND THE SYRUP.

ZABAGLIONE

FOR EACH PERSON:
1 EGG YOLK
1 TABLESPOON CASTOR SUGAR
2 TABLESPOONS MARSALA OR
** WHITE WINE**

FLAVOURING:
1 TABLESPOON OF ZEST OF EITHER
** LEMON OR ORANGE, OR**
1 TABLESPOON OF VANILLA OR
** CHOICE OF LIQUEUR**

PLACE ALL INGREDIENTS IN THE TOP OF A
DOUBLE BOILER.
BEAT WITH WHISK UNTIL FROTHY AND CREAMY.
CONTINUE TO BEAT UNTIL THICK, LIGHT AND FLUFFY.

ZABAGLIONE CAN BE FLAVOURED WITH ORANGE OR
LEMON ZEST OR VANILLA OR A LIQUEUR.
IT CAN BE SERVED HOT OR COLD. TO SERVE COLD
CONTINUE TO BEAT OVER ICE UNTIL COLD.
SERVE IN GLASSES WITH A BISCUIT.

ICARUS, KNOWN IN LEGEND AS HAVING FLOWN
TOO CLOSE TO ZABAGLIONE

LEMON GELATO

375ml/1 1/2 CUPS LEMON JUICE
375ml/1 1/2 CUPS WHITE WINE
300g/1 1/2 CUPS CASTOR SUGAR
375ml/1 1/2 CUPS WATER
3 EGG WHITES
ZEST OF 1/2 LEMON

HEAT WINE, SUGAR AND WATER, STIRRING UNTIL SUGAR IS DISSOLVED.

BOIL, THEN REDUCE HEAT AND SIMMER FOR 10 MINUTES.

COOL.

STRAIN LEMON JUICE AND STIR INTO MIXTURE.

ADD ZEST AND MIX THROUGH WELL.

POUR INTO A SHALLOW TRAY AND PLACE IN FREEZER UNTIL MIXTURE IS FIRM (ABOUT 1 HOUR).

REMOVE FROM FREEZER AND PUT IN A METAL BOWL.

BEAT UNTIL SMOOTH.

WHISK EGG WHITES UNTIL THEY FORM PEAKS, AND FOLD THROUGH MIXTURE.

RETURN TO TRAY AND FREEZE UNTIL FIRM.

SERVE IN GLASS BOWLS OR CHAMPAGNE GLASSES.

RICOTTA PIE WITH CHOCOLATE AND AMARETTO

PASTRY:

320g/11oz PLAIN FLOUR

3 EGG YOLKS

100g/4oz UNSALTED BUTTER

80g/3oz CASTOR SUGAR

COMBINE ALL INGREDIENTS, MIXING INTO A DOUGH.
SHAPE INTO A FLATTISH DISK SHAPE.
REST IN REFRIGERATOR.

FILLING:

3 EGG YOLKS

80g/3oz WHITE SUGAR

2 TABLESPOONS FLOUR

250ml/1 CUP MILK

90g/3oz PLAIN, DARK CHOCOLATE

4 TABLESPOONS AMARETTO LIQUEUR

250g/9oz RICOTTA CHEESE

PINCH OF CINNAMON

GRATED RIND OF 1 ORANGE

1 EGG WHITE

BEAT EGG YOLKS WITH SUGAR UNTIL FLUFFY.

ADD FLOUR AND MILK AND COOK OVER DOUBLE

BOILER UNTIL THICKENED.

MELT CHOCOLATE WITH AMARETTO LIQUEUR,
STIR INTO EGG MIXTURE AND LEAVE TO COOL.

SIEVE RICOTTA.

GRADUALLY ADD EGG MIXTURE, CINNAMON
AND ORANGE ZEST.

MIX WELL AND SET ASIDE.

PREHEAT OVEN TO 180°C/350°F/GAS MARK 4.

BUTTER AND FLOUR A 25cm PIE TIN. ROLL OUT $^2/_3$
OF THE DOUGH AND LINE THE TIN WITH IT.

USE REMAINING PASTRY FOR THE TOP.
POUR IN THE FILLING.

COVER WITH THE REMAINING PASTRY. CRIMP EDGES
AND BRUSH TOP WITH BEATEN EGG WHITE.

BAKE 40 MINUTES, UNTIL CRUST IS GOLDEN BROWN.

COOL.

DUST WITH ICING SUGAR BEFORE SERVING.

SERVE WITH WHIPPED CREAM.

MEANINGLESS ILLUSTRATION

ANTIPASTO

CAULIFLOWER WITH MOZZARELLA

1 MEDIUM CAULIFLOWER

2 ANCHOVIES

250ml/1 CUP OLIVE OIL

1 MEDIUM ONION, FINELY CHOPPED

12 BLACK OLIVES, PITTED

60g/2oz SLICED MOZZARELLA

250ml/1 CUP RED WINE

SALT AND PEPPER

SEPARATE CAULIFLOWER INTO FLORETS.

WASH AND CHOP THE ANCHOVIES.

POUR 3 TABLESPOONS OLIVE OIL INTO A
CASSEROLE DISH.

LAYER ONIONS, OLIVES, ANCHOVIES, FLORETS OF
CAULIFLOWER AND MOZZARELLA. REPEAT, SPRINKLING
WITH OIL, SALT AND PEPPER.

ADD WINE, COVER CASSEROLE.

COOK UNTIL TENDER. SERVE IN CASSEROLE.

ROCKMELON WITH PROSCIUTTO

1 ROCKMELON (CHILLED)
12 SLICES PROSCIUTTO

CUT ROCKMELON IN HALF. SCOOP OUT SEEDS.

SLICE EACH HALF INTO SIX EQUAL SLICES.

CUT OFF SKIN.

DRAPE PROSCIUTTO OVER ROCKMELON SLICES.

SERVE IMMEDIATELY WITH FRESHLY GROUND
BLACK PEPPER.

STEWED GLOBE ARTICHOKES AND FAVA BEANS

6 ARTICHOKES
JUICE OF 1 LEMON
125ml/^{1}/$_2$ CUP OLIVE OIL
1 MEDIUM ONION, FINELY CHOPPED
1 400g/14oz CAN
FAVA BEANS/BROAD BEANS
2 TABLESPOONS CHOPPED PARSLEY
PINCH OF NUTMEG
200ml/^{3}/$_4$ CUP HOT WATER
SALT AND PEPPER

TRIM ARTICHOKES AND REMOVE CHOKE.

CUT IN HALF AND THEN INTO THREE.

PLACE IN WATER ACIDULATED WITH THE LEMON JUICE.

HEAT OIL IN POT AND SAUTE ONION UNTIL SOFT OVER MEDIUM HEAT.

ADD ARTICHOKES AND HOT WATER.

BRING TO BOIL AND SIMMER FOR 20 MINUTES.

ADD FAVA BEANS, NUTMEG AND SALT AND PEPPER.

ADD EXTRA WATER IF NECESSARY.

SIMMER 5 MINUTES.

SERVE HOT OR COLD SPRINKLED WITH CHOPPED PARSLEY.

ZUCCHINI, CAPSICUM AND MUSHROOM FRITTATA

100g/1 CUP ZUCCHINI/COURGETTE, THINLY SLICED

100g/1 CUP CAPSICUM, THINLY SLICED

50g/1 CUP MUSHROOMS, THINLY SLICED

6 WHOLE EGGS

3 TABLESPOONS PARMESAN OR PECORINO, GRATED

2 TABLESPOONS MEDIUM-HARD CHEESE (GRUYERE)

3 TABLESPOONS OLIVE OIL

1 TABLESPOON CHOPPED BASIL

1 TABLESPOON CHOPPED PARSLEY

SALT AND PEPPER

HEAT OLIVE OIL IN A NON-STICK FRYING PAN.

ADD VEGETABLES, SAUTE UNTIL SOFT.

BEAT EGGS IN BOWL.

SEASON AND ADD CHOPPED HERBS.

ADD CHEESE. POUR THE MIXTURE OVER VEGETABLES.

COOK OVER LOW HEAT UNTIL THE FRITTATA STARTS TO SET.

FLIP FRITTATA OVER AND COOK TOP.

WHEN COOLED, SLIDE ONTO PLATE AND ALLOW TO COOL SLIGHTLY BEFORE CUTTING INTO SLICES

MARINATED SARDINES

6 MEDIUM SARDINES (FRESH), HEADS OFF, GUTTED

6 TABLESPOONS OLIVE OIL

100g/4oz PLAIN FLOUR

SALT AND PEPPER

6 TABLESPOONS WHITE WINE VINEGAR

7 BAY LEAVES

2 TABLESPOONS CHOPPED PARSLEY

WASH SARDINES. PAT DRY WITH PAPER TOWEL.

DREDGE SARDINES IN FLOUR. HEAT OIL IN FRYING PAN OVER MEDIUM HEAT. WHEN HOT ADD SARDINES.

INCREASE HEAT AND FRY UNTIL GOLDEN. TURN AND REPEAT.

SEASON.

ARRANGE IN A SERVING DISH IN A SINGLE LAYER.

PLACE ONIONS IN FRYING PAN, TURN HEAT TO LOW.

COOK UNTIL SOFT. ADD VINEGAR, TURN UP HEAT TO SIMMER.

POUR OVER FISH. PLACE BAY LEAVES ON TOP. LEAVE TO MARINATE FOR 4 HOURS.

SERVE AT ROOM TEMPERATURE WITH CHOPPED PARSLEY SCATTERED OVER TOP.

ITALIAN INGREDIENTS

GARLIC – IS USED DIFFERENTLY IN DIFFERENT REGIONS OF ITALY. IT IS USED IN SAUCES AND TO FLAVOUR OLIVE OIL.

CHOPPED FINELY AND SERVED RAW AS AN ACCOMPANIMENT TO A DISH – EITHER IN OLIVE OIL OR ON ITS OWN.

SERVED ON BRUSCHETTA WITH OLIVE OIL, ROASTED, FRIED.

GARLIC OIL – SLIGHTLY CRUSH 6-8 CLOVES GARLIC (PRE-PEELED) AND COVER WITH 125ml/$^1/_2$ CUP OLIVE OIL.

ADD SALT, LET STAND SEVERAL HOURS. STRAIN BEFORE USING. THIS OIL WILL KEEP FOR SEVERAL MONTHS IN THE REFRIGERATOR.

HERBS – THE MAIN ITALIAN HERBS ARE PARSLEY, BASIL, OREGANO, SAGE, MINT, MARJORAM AND BAY LEAVES.

OTHER HERBS USED INCLUDE THYME, TARRAGON, CHIVES, JUNIPER AND ROSEMARY.

OLIVE OIL IS USED IN ITALY AS A CONDIMENT ON THE TABLE – TO BE POURED OVER ANY AND EVERYTHING. THERE ARE 4 MAIN TYPES: EXTRA VIRGIN, WHICH IS A DARK GREEN, STRONG, FRUITY OIL, MADE FROM THE FIRST OLIVE PRESSING; VIRGIN OIL FROM THE SECOND PRESSING IS A MEDIUM GREEN, MODERATE-TASTING OIL; PURE OIL HAS THE FLAVOUR EXTRACTED, IT IS STRAW-COLOURED AND CAN BE A LITTLE BITTER; AND FINE OLIVE OIL, AN OIL PROCESSED

FURTHER WHICH IS NOT RECOMMENDED.
THE ITALIANS USE A PURE OR LIGHT OIL FOR
COOKING AND A VIRGIN OR EXTRA VIRGIN OIL
FOR ACCOMPANYING A DISH AND ENHANCING
ITS FLAVOUR.
IT IS A GOOD IDEA TO DO AN OLIVE OIL TASTING TO
CHOOSE FOR YOURSELF THE FLAVOUR YOU REQUIRE,
OR BUY FROM STORES WHICH SPECIALISE IN ITALIAN
PRODUCTS AND ASK FOR THEIR RECOMMENDATION.
STORE AWAY FROM THE HEAT AND LIGHT.

VINEGAR – RED WINE, BALSAMIC AND WHITE WINE
ARE THE PRIMARY VINEGARS. FOR THOSE WHO ARE
LESS OF A PURIST, YOU CAN PLAY AROUND WITH A
VARIETY OF FLAVOURED VINEGARS. BALSAMIC IS A
RICH, WARM FLAVOURED, SWEETER VINEGAR, BUT DUE
TO ITS COLOUR CAN 'MUDDY' A SALAD.

CAN BE USED TO DEGLAZE MEAT DISHES AND ON
FISH. ALWAYS USE QUALITY VINEGARS.

CAPERS – RINSE BEFORE USING. CAPERS ADD AN
EARTHY TANG TO DISHES. CAPERS LAST IN YOUR
REFRIGERATOR INDEFINITELY.

ILLUSTRATION FULL OF MEANING

ANCHOVIES OFTEN FOUND IN ITALIAN RECIPES, ANCHOVIES ARE NOT SO MUCH A FEATURE AS A FLAVOUR ENHANCER. WHEN USED IN MODERATION, THERE IS NO NOTICEABLE 'FISHY' TASTE, BUT JUST THAT DEPTH OF FLAVOUR SO IMPORTANT IN ITALIAN FOOD. WHEN USING TINNED ANCHOVIES, RINSE THEM UNDER COLD WATER FIRST, THEN STAND FOR ONE HOUR IN MILK. THIS SOFTENS THE ANCHOVIES AND TAKES AWAY SOME OF THE SALTINESS. RINSE AGAIN BEFORE USING.

CAPSICUMS HAVE BECOME IDENTIFIED WITH ITALIAN COOKING. THEY COME IN 3 MAIN COLOURS – WITH VARIATIONS OF THESE FOUND, E.G., LIGHTER OR DARKER HUES OF THE MAJOR COLOURS, GREEN, RED AND YELLOW.

ROASTING THE PEPPERS ADDS A SLIGHTLY SWEET, SMOKY FLAVOUR TO ANTIPASTO PLATES.

TO ROAST, PLACE UNDER THE GRILLER AND CHAR ON EACH SIDE. PLACE IN A PLASTIC OR PAPER BAG FOR 30 MINUTES TO 1 HOUR. PEEL SKIN AWAY AND DISCARD SEEDS AND CORE.

PICK-UP ARRANGEMENTS IN AN ITALIAN CAFE

CHEESE

TASTE BEFORE YOU BUY. CHEESES ARE A PERFECT ACCOMPANIMENT TO ANY ALFRESCO DISH OR SNACK. ADD TO A PLATTER OF CRUSTY BREAD, OLIVES, ROASTED CAPSICUMS OR EGGPLANTS WITH A DISH OF OLIVE OIL ON THE SIDE (FOR DUNKING!). GREAT FOR THOSE IMPROMPTU ANTIPASTOS. THOUGH THERE ARE MANY GREAT ITALIAN CHEESES, LISTED BELOW ARE A FEW EXAMPLES:

BEL PAESE – A SOFT, MILD CHEESE. CREAMY WITH A SLIGHT TANG. ADDS A GREAT RICH TEXTURE TO COOKING.

GORGONZOLA – A BLUE–VEINED, STRONG-FLAVOURED CHEESE.

MOZZARELLA IS MADE IN SOUTHERN ITALY FROM THE MILK OF A WATER BUFFALO. IT IS A BLAND, MILKY CHEESE, SOFT BUT FIRM IN TEXTURE. BOCCONCINIS ARE THE SMALLEST MOZZARELLAS AND THEY ARE VERY WHITE AND MILKY. GREAT SERVED WITH TOMATOES, BASIL, OLIVE OIL, SALT, CRACKED PEPPER AND GARLIC.

MASCARPONE IS A VERY SOFT, FRESH CREAMY CHEESE MADE FROM COWS' MILK. IT CAN BE BEATEN WITH FRUIT OR BEATEN WITH A LIQUEUR AND EGG YOLKS AND SUGAR.

PARMIGIANO REGGIANO IS ONE OF THE GREATEST CHEESES, DATING BACK 2,500 YEARS. A CRUMBLY, MILDLY SALTY, WHEAT-COLOURED CHEESE. STRONG FLAVOUR.
IS USED AS A GRATED CHEESE IN STUFFINGS, FILLINGS, OVER THE TOPS OF MEAT AND FISH DISHES, AND VEGETABLE AND PASTA DISHES. GREAT GRATED OVER SOUPS. THE CHEESE ENHANCES THE FLAVOUR OF THESE DISHES. KEEP IT IN THE FRIDGE IN A SINGLE PIECE AND GRATE ONLY AS NEEDED.

RICOTTA IS A WHEY CHEESE. A MOIST, SOFT, MILKY, UNSALTED CHEESE. IT MUST BE EATEN FRESH, AND IS GREAT SERVED WITH FIGS OR MORTADELLA.

TOMATOES – ORIGINALLY BELIEVED TO BE A POISONOUS PLANT, THE ITALIANS WERE THE FIRST EUROPEANS TO ACCEPT IT AS EDIBLE, AND NOW, IN ONE WAY OR ANOTHER, TOMATOES ARE PART OF MOST OF THEIR DISHES. IF TOMATOES ARE NOT IN SEASON DO NOT SUBSTITUTE PALE, WATERY ONES. INSTEAD, USE A CAN OF GOOD, RICH ITALIAN TOMATOES. OBVIOUSLY THESE CAN NOT BE USED IN SALADS – SO SAVE THE SALADS FOR TOMATO SEASON!

SUN-DRIED TOMATOES ARE DEHYDRATED TOMATOES, DRIED IN THE OPEN AIR. THEY HAVE A SALTY, PIQUANT FLAVOUR AND ARE USUALLY STORED IN OLIVE OIL. A GREAT ADDITION TO ANTIPASTO; CAN BE ADDED TO SALADS; OR CAN BE EATEN ON THEIR OWN WITH CHEESE AND CRUSTY BREAD.

COLD MEATS

PANCETTA – THE EQUIVALENT OF BACON,
BUT NOT SMOKED.

PROSCIUTTO – A CURED RAW ITALIAN HAM.
IT HAS SALT AND PEPPER ENCRUSTED AROUND
THE OUTSIDE AND IS AIR-DRIED, PRESSED AND AGED.
IT SHOULD HAVE A SWEET, RICH FLAVOUR AND BE
SLICED THINLY. IT IS FAMOUS AS PART OF ANTIPASTO,
SERVED WITH MELON OR FIGS. IT IS ALSO USED IN
MANY COOKED DISHES – PASTAS, STUFFINGS,
SAUCES, SOUPS, STEWS AND VEGETABLES.
IT IS A SALTY MEAT, SO WHEN USED IN A DISH,
TASTE BEFORE ADDING SALT.

ANOTHER MEANINGLESS ILLUSTRATION